EXCUSE ME WHILE I PANIC

1998 DESK CALENDAR

DILBERT™

BY SCOTT ADAMS

Andrews McMeel Publishing

an Andrews McMeel Universal company
Kansas City

 For information, write Andrews McMeel Publishing, an Andrews McMeel Universal company, 4520 Main Street, Kansas City, Missouri 64111.

ISBN: 0-8362-3151-1

E-Mail: SCOTTADAMS@AOL.COM

Are you interested in receiving the official publication of DOGBERT'S NEW RULING CLASS (the DNRC)?

It's FREE! Subscribe automatically via e-mail:

Address: LISTSERV@listserv.unitedmedia.com
Subject: Newsletter
Message: SUBSCRIBE Dilbert_News YourFirstName YourLastName
(Fill in your first and last name only)

Or send your name and address to:

THE DILBERT NEWSLETTER
c/o United Media
200 Madison Avenue
New York, NY 10016

1998

January

S	M	T	W	T	F	S
				1	2	3
4	5	6	7	8	9	10
11	12	13	14	15	16	17
18	19	20	21	22	23	24
25	26	27	28	29	30	31

February

S	M	T	W	T	F	S
1	2	3	4	5	6	7
8	9	10	11	12	13	14
15	16	17	18	19	20	21
22	23	24	25	26	27	28

March

S	M	T	W	T	F	S
1	2	3	4	5	6	7
8	9	10	11	12	13	14
15	16	17	18	19	20	21
22	23	24	25	26	27	28
29	30	31				

April

S	M	T	W	T	F	S
			1	2	3	4
5	6	7	8	9	10	11
12	13	14	15	16	17	18
19	20	21	22	23	24	25
26	27	28	29	30		

May

S	M	T	W	T	F	S
					1	2
3	4	5	6	7	8	9
10	11	12	13	14	15	16
17	18	19	20	21	22	23
24	25	26	27	28	29	30
31						

June

S	M	T	W	T	F	S
	1	2	3	4	5	6
7	8	9	10	11	12	13
14	15	16	17	18	19	20
21	22	23	24	25	26	27
28	29	30				

July

S	M	T	W	T	F	S
			1	2	3	4
5	6	7	8	9	10	11
12	13	14	15	16	17	18
19	20	21	22	23	24	25
26	27	28	29	30	31	

August

S	M	T	W	T	F	S
						1
2	3	4	5	6	7	8
9	10	11	12	13	14	15
16	17	18	19	20	21	22
23	24	25	26	27	28	29
30	31					

September

S	M	T	W	T	F	S
		1	2	3	4	5
6	7	8	9	10	11	12
13	14	15	16	17	18	19
20	21	22	23	24	25	26
27	28	29	30			

October

S	M	T	W	T	F	S
				1	2	3
4	5	6	7	8	9	10
11	12	13	14	15	16	17
18	19	20	21	22	23	24
25	26	27	28	29	30	31

November

S	M	T	W	T	F	S
1	2	3	4	5	6	7
8	9	10	11	12	13	14
15	16	17	18	19	20	21
22	23	24	25	26	27	28
29	30					

December

S	M	T	W	T	F	S
		1	2	3	4	5
6	7	8	9	10	11	12
13	14	15	16	17	18	19
20	21	22	23	24	25	26
27	28	29	30	31		

I PUT TOGETHER A TIME LINE FOR YOUR PROJECT.
I STARTED BY REASONING THAT ANYTHING I DON'T UNDERSTAND IS EASY TO DO.
PHASE ONE: DESIGN A CLIENT-SERVER ARCHITECTURE FOR OUR WORLD-WIDE OPERATIONS. TIME: SIX MINUTES.
© 1994 United Feature Syndicate, Inc.

AVOID AT ALL COSTS . . .

DEC 29-JAN 4

29
MONDAY

30
TUESDAY

31
WEDNESDAY

1
THURSDAY

New Year's Day

2
FRIDAY

3
SATURDAY

4
SUNDAY

DECEMBER 1997

S	M	T	W	T	F	S
	1	2	3	4	5	6
7	8	9	10	11	12	13
14	15	16	17	18	19	20
21	22	23	24	25	26	27
28	29	30	31			

JANUARY

S	M	T	W	T	F	S
				1	2	3
4	5	6	7	8	9	10
11	12	13	14	15	16	17
18	19	20	21	22	23	24
25	26	27	28	29	30	31

DOGBERT'S TECH SUPPORT
I THINK I KNOW WHAT YOUR PROBLEM IS...
S. Adams
TAKE ALL THE PARTS AND ARRANGE THEM IN NEAT PILES. NOW STAND ON YOUR CHAIR SO YOU CAN SEE ABOVE YOUR CUBICLE WALL...
11-30
© 1994 United Feature Syndicate, Inc.
NOW SHOUT "DOES ANYBODY KNOW HOW TO READ A MANUAL?"

DOGBERT's New Ruling Class

When DOGBERT conquers the world, he'll make everyone his servants except the official members of his new ruling class. As such, non-members (or "Induhviduals") will be treated with the same courtesy and respect as five-and-a-quarter-inch diskettes.

Actual Titles Awarded to DNRC Members:

Supreme Arch Techno-Weenie

Lord High Everything Else

Lifeguard of the Internet

Supreme Overlord of the Waffle Light

Judge of Wedgies

HOW **MY** WEEK IS GOING . . .

JANUARY 5-11

5 MONDAY

6 TUESDAY

7 WEDNESDAY

8 THURSDAY

9 FRIDAY

10 SATURDAY

11 SUNDAY

JANUARY

S	M	T	W	T	F	S
				1	2	3
4	5	6	7	8	9	10
11	12	13	14	15	16	17
18	19	20	21	22	23	24
25	26	27	28	29	30	31

LET'S GO AROUND THE TABLE AND GIVE AN UPDATE ON EACH OF OUR PROJECTS.
S. Adams
1-10
MY PROJECT IS A PATHETIC SERIES OF POORLY PLANNED, NEAR-RANDOM ACTS. MY LIFE IS A TRAGEDY OF EMOTIONAL DESPERATION.
IT'S MORE OR LESS CUSTOMARY TO SAY THINGS ARE GOING FINE.
I THINK I NEED A HUG.

DAY FILLER . . .

JANUARY
12-18

12
MONDAY

13
TUESDAY

14
WEDNESDAY

15
THURSDAY

16
FRIDAY

17
SATURDAY

18
SUNDAY

JANUARY

S	M	T	W	T	F	S
				1	2	3
4	5	6	7	8	9	10
11	12	13	14	15	16	17
18	19	20	21	22	23	24
25	26	27	28	29	30	31

I WANT YOU TO STUDY OUR OPTIONS FOR PROJECT "ZEBRA" AND MAKE A RECOMMENDATION.
TRANSLATION: "READ MY MIND THEN RECOMMEND THE OPTION I'VE ALREADY DECIDED ON."
S.Adams
7/15 © 1995 United Feature Syndicate, Inc. (NYC)
I'LL GET RIGHT ON IT!
TRANSLATION: "I AM DOOMED. I WILL GO LOOK FOR NAUGHTY PICTURES ON THE INTERNET INSTEAD."

WORKING HARDER, NOT SMARTER . . .

JANUARY 19-25

19
MONDAY

Martin Luther King Jr.'s Birthday (observed)

20
TUESDAY

21
WEDNESDAY

22
THURSDAY

23
FRIDAY

24
SATURDAY

25
SUNDAY

JANUARY

S	M	T	W	T	F	S
				1	2	3
4	5	6	7	8	9	10
11	12	13	14	15	16	17
18	19	20	21	22	23	24
25	26	27	28	29	30	31

LACKING CLERICAL SUPPORT, THE HIGHLY TRAINED, HIGHLY PAID PROFESSIONALS LINE UP AT THE COPIER.
S.ADAMS
THEIR AMAZING ANALYTICAL SKILLS ARE SQUANDERED IN THIS MINDLESS TASK.
6/15 © 1995 United Feature Syndicate, Inc. (NYC)
NO... IT LOOKS LIKE THE "TONER" LIGHT DOESN'T TURN OFF IF YOU WAIT.
LET'S GIVE IT ANOTHER FIVE MINUTES.

PLANS FOR WORLD DOMINATION . . .

JAN 26-
FEB 1

26
MONDAY

27
TUESDAY

28
WEDNESDAY

29
THURSDAY

30
FRIDAY

31
SATURDAY

1
SUNDAY

JANUARY

S	M	T	W	T	F	S
				1	2	3
4	5	6	7	8	9	10
11	12	13	14	15	16	17
18	19	20	21	22	23	24
25	26	27	28	29	30	31

FEBRUARY

S	M	T	W	T	F	S
1	2	3	4	5	6	7
8	9	10	11	12	13	14
15	16	17	18	19	20	21
22	23	24	25	26	27	28

THE LESS YOU KNOW, THE HAPPIER YOU ARE.
S. Adams
WHILE YOU STRUGGLE WITH THAT COMPUTER, I'M NAKED, CLUELESS, AND F-E-E-E-LING GOOD!
1-29
YOU'RE REALLY ANNOYING ME NOW.
TOTALLY NAKED! ISN'T THAT A HOOT?

OH, YEAH . . .

FEBRUARY 2-8

2 MONDAY

Groundhog Day

3 TUESDAY

4 WEDNESDAY

5 THURSDAY

6 FRIDAY

7 SATURDAY

8 SUNDAY

FEBRUARY

S	M	T	W	T	F	S
1	2	3	4	5	6	7
8	9	10	11	12	13	14
15	16	17	18	19	20	21
22	23	24	25	26	27	28

I CAN TELL THAT YOU LIKE ME BECAUSE YOU DON'T QUITE KNOW WHAT TO DO WITH YOUR HANDS.
6-25
S. Adams
TO TEST MY HYPOTHESIS I WILL HOLD THIS HAND AND OBSERVE THE CHANGE.
© 1994 United Feature Syndicate, Inc.
THE "CONTROL" HAND REMAINS LIMP AND CLAMMY. ITS TWIN LOSES CONTROL. HYPOTHESIS CONFIRMED.
THUPA THUPA THUPA THUPA THUPA THUPA

DOGBERT Answers My Mail

Dear Mister Adams:

We are students at Dartmouth. We keep reading your strip and can't find any humor there. Is it supposed to be funny or autobiographical or what?

—Timmy and Ron

Dear Timmy and Ron:

I'll bet you have athletic scholarships.

—DOGBERT

HOOPS TO JUMP THROUGH . . .

FEBRUARY
9-15

9
MONDAY

10
TUESDAY

11
WEDNESDAY

12
THURSDAY

13
FRIDAY

14
SATURDAY

Valentine's Day

15
SUNDAY

FEBRUARY

S	M	T	W	T	F	S
1	2	3	4	5	6	7
8	9	10	11	12	13	14
15	16	17	18	19	20	21
22	23	24	25	26	27	28

YOU'VE GOT TO INCREASE THE BUDGET FOR TRAINING!
S.ADAMS
IF I TRAIN YOU, THEN WOULDN'T YOU JUST LEAVE THE COMPANY TO MAKE MORE MONEY WORKING FOR OUR COMPETITOR?
6/10 © 1995 United Feature Syndicate, Inc. (NYC)
I GUESS THERE IS A DOWN-SIDE.
AND THE DOWNSIDE WOULD BE...?

BRAINSTORM . . .

FEBRUARY 16-22

16
MONDAY

Presidents' Day

17
TUESDAY

18
WEDNESDAY

19
THURSDAY

20
FRIDAY

21
SATURDAY

22
SUNDAY

FEBRUARY

S	M	T	W	T	F	S
1	2	3	4	5	6	7
8	9	10	11	12	13	14
15	16	17	18	19	20	21
22	23	24	25	26	27	28

IN THIS SENSITIVITY EXERCISE, CLOSE YOUR EYES AND IMAGINE HOW IT FEELS TO BE A WOMAN.
S. Adams
6-3
PEOPLE ACKNOWLEDGE MY EXISTENCE. THEY SMILE FOR NO REASON AND HOLD THE DOOR OPEN. I'M... I'M POPULAR.
I CAN'T FIND MY KEYS.
© 1994 United Feature Syndicate, Inc.
I'M NEVER GOING BACK. I CAN'T. I WON'T.
MY BLOUSE FALLS TO THE FLOOR...
BREAK! BREAK!

DUE WHEN?

FEB 23-MAR 1

23
MONDAY

24
TUESDAY

25
WEDNESDAY

Ash Wednesday

26
THURSDAY

27
FRIDAY

28
SATURDAY

1
SUNDAY

FEBRUARY

S	M	T	W	T	F	S
1	2	3	4	5	6	7
8	9	10	11	12	13	14
15	16	17	18	19	20	21
22	23	24	25	26	27	28

MARCH

S	M	T	W	T	F	S
1	2	3	4	5	6	7
8	9	10	11	12	13	14
15	16	17	18	19	20	21
22	23	24	25	26	27	28
29	30	31				

ALICE, I WANT YOU TO BENCHMARK THESE WORLD-CLASS COMPANIES. FIND OUT HOW WE COMPARE.
S. Adams
I'M BETTING THEY DON'T MAKE VERBS OUT OF NOUNS. AND I'LL BET THEY DON'T ASSIGN ENGINEERS TO DO FIELD RESEARCH.
6/27 © 1995 United Feature Syndicate, Inc. (NYC)
DO YOU GUYS HAVE ANY POINTY-HAIRED IDIOTS RUNNING YOUR PLACE?
WOULD YOU LIKE ONE?

UH-OH . . .

MARCH
2-8

2
MONDAY

3
TUESDAY

4
WEDNESDAY

5
THURSDAY

6
FRIDAY

7
SATURDAY

8
SUNDAY

MARCH

S	M	T	W	T	F	S
1	2	3	4	5	6	7
8	9	10	11	12	13	14
15	16	17	18	19	20	21
22	23	24	25	26	27	28
29	30	31				

I'VE GIVEN UP ON THE WHOLE DATING SCENE. I'VE DECIDED TO REPRODUCE BY ASEXUAL CELL DIVISION.
S. Adams
I DIDN'T REALIZE THAT WAS AN OPTION.
YOU NEVER KNOW UNTIL YOU TRY.
10-15
© 1994 United Feature Syndicate, Inc.
I THINK I'LL STEER CLEAR OF HERE FOR A WHILE.
DIVIDE! DIVIDE!

Most Frequently Asked Question

Why does DILBERT's tie curl up like that?

The answer is either A) It's a metaphor for his inability to control his environment or B) He's just glad to see you.

—S.A.

FOR A BETTER LIFE . . .

MARCH 9-15

9
MONDAY

10
TUESDAY

11
WEDNESDAY

12
THURSDAY

Purim

13
FRIDAY

14
SATURDAY

15
SUNDAY

MARCH

S	M	T	W	T	F	S
1	2	3	4	5	6	7
8	9	10	11	12	13	14
15	16	17	18	19	20	21
22	23	24	25	26	27	28
29	30	31				

I'M SORRY DAVE, BUT YOU'RE BEING TRANS-FERRED TO MARKETING AND THERE'S NO BUDGET TO TRAIN YOU AS A MARKETER.
S. Adams
SLAP!
1-3-94
WHERE AM I? I NEED A DRINK:
THIS IS A TEMPORARY FIX... BUT YOU'LL FIT IN NOW.

MEETINGS TO POSTPONE . . .

MARCH 16-22

16
MONDAY

17
TUESDAY

St. Patrick's Day

18
WEDNESDAY

19
THURSDAY

20
FRIDAY

21
SATURDAY

22
SUNDAY

MARCH

S	M	T	W	T	F	S
1	2	3	4	5	6	7
8	9	10	11	12	13	14
15	16	17	18	19	20	21
22	23	24	25	26	27	28
29	30	31				

TELL ME ABOUT YOUR PROJECT AND I'LL TRANSLATE IT INTO WEASEL WORDS FOR THE BUSINESS CASE.
S. Adams
WELL... AN EXECUTIVE HAD LUNCH WITH A VENDOR AND COMMITTED TO BUY SOME STUFF THAT DOESN'T WORK. OUR JOB IS TO COST-JUSTIFY THE DECISION.
4-13
I QUIT.
DON'T GET ALL ETHICAL ON US.

ON-LINE THIS WEEK . . .

MARCH 23-29

23
MONDAY

24
TUESDAY

25
WEDNESDAY

26
THURSDAY

27
FRIDAY

28
SATURDAY

29
SUNDAY

MARCH

S	M	T	W	T	F	S
1	2	3	4	5	6	7
8	9	10	11	12	13	14
15	16	17	18	19	20	21
22	23	24	25	26	27	28
29	30	31				

THIS DESKTOP VIDEO CONFERENCE THING IS GREAT!
EVEN THOUGH YOU'RE TELECOMMUTING, YOU STILL MAINTAIN A LEVEL OF PROFESSIONALISM.
LET'S SHARE A DOCUMENT NEXT TIME.
© 1994 United Feature Syndicate, Inc.

I'M SUPPOSED TO REMEMBER . . .

MAR 30-APR 5

30 MONDAY

31 TUESDAY

1 WEDNESDAY

2 THURSDAY

3 FRIDAY

4 SATURDAY

5 SUNDAY

Palm Sunday

MARCH

S	M	T	W	T	F	S
1	2	3	4	5	6	7
8	9	10	11	12	13	14
15	16	17	18	19	20	21
22	23	24	25	26	27	28
29	30	31				

APRIL

S	M	T	W	T	F	S
			1	2	3	4
5	6	7	8	9	10	11
12	13	14	15	16	17	18
19	20	21	22	23	24	25
26	27	28	29	30		

RATBERT THE TEMP WORKER
THIS IS REALLY TESTING MY SENSE OF SELF-WORTH.
S.Adams
I WILL COMPENSATE BY SHOUTING A LIST OF MY TALENTS TO ANYBODY WHO WALKS PAST.
8/4 © 1995 United Feature Syndicate, Inc. (NYC)
IGNORE HIM. HE'S TRYING TO TRICK US INTO MAKING EYE CONTACT.
I EAT RUBBER! I CARRY DISEASE! I ENJOY OPERA!

LADDERS TO CLIMB . . .

APRIL 6-12

6
MONDAY

7
TUESDAY

8
WEDNESDAY

9
THURSDAY

10
FRIDAY

Good Friday

11
SATURDAY

Passover

12
SUNDAY

Easter

APRIL

S	M	T	W	T	F	S
			1	2	3	4
5	6	7	8	9	10	11
12	13	14	15	16	17	18
19	20	21	22	23	24	25
26	27	28	29	30		

I'M REORGANIZING THE DEPARTMENT INTO FAST-MOVING TEAMS.
GOOD PLAN. WE'LL NEVER REALIZE WE'RE POWERLESS, MICRO-MANAGED SERFS AFTER WE CALL OURSELVES A "TEAM."
S. Adams
8/11 © 1995 United Feature Syndicate, Inc. (NYC)
I NEED SOME LESS EXPERIENCED PEOPLE.
I FEEL FASTER ALREADY.
THE G-FORCES ARE KILLING ME.

Tax Little Billy!

I support a law that would tax readers of "Family Circus" and give the money to DNRC members. I think we could argue that it stimulates the economy since we would be inclined to go out and blow any extra money we got, whereas "Family Circus" readers would just squirrel it away in a mattress in the attic until rats ate it.

—S.A.

WHAT PROJECT?

APRIL 13-19

13
MONDAY

Easter Monday (Canada)

14
TUESDAY

15
WEDNESDAY

16
THURSDAY

17
FRIDAY

18
SATURDAY

19
SUNDAY

APRIL

S	M	T	W	T	F	S
			1	2	3	4
5	6	7	8	9	10	11
12	13	14	15	16	17	18
19	20	21	22	23	24	25
26	27	28	29	30		

WE'RE FLATTENING THE ORGANIZATION TO ELIMINATE LEVELS AND PUT EVERYBODY IN A WIDE SALARY BAND.
S.Adams
NOW INSTEAD OF NOT GETTING A PROMOTION YOU'LL ONLY NOT GET A RAISE.
1-5-94
© 1993 United Feature Syndicate, Inc.
SO, WHAT JOB TITLE DO WE USE?
YOU'LL ALL BE NAMED BEVERLY.

PRETEND TO DO . . .

APRIL 20-26

20 MONDAY

21 TUESDAY

22 WEDNESDAY

23 THURSDAY

24 FRIDAY

25 SATURDAY

26 SUNDAY

APRIL

S	M	T	W	T	F	S
			1	2	3	4
5	6	7	8	9	10	11
12	13	14	15	16	17	18
19	20	21	22	23	24	25
26	27	28	29	30		

ALICE, I'VE DECIDED TO ADD A RESOURCE TO YOUR PROJECT.
WE'RE HUMAN BEINGS, NOT "RESOURCES"!!
WOULD IT HELP IF I TOLD YOU THAT RESOURCES ARE OUR MOST VALUABLE ASSET?
S. Adams
9/22 © 1995 United Feature Syndicate, Inc.(NYC)

I JUST REALIZED . . .

APRIL 27-MAY 3

27 MONDAY

28 TUESDAY

29 WEDNESDAY

30 THURSDAY

1 FRIDAY

2 SATURDAY

3 SUNDAY

APRIL

S	M	T	W	T	F	S
			1	2	3	4
5	6	7	8	9	10	11
12	13	14	15	16	17	18
19	20	21	22	23	24	25
26	27	28	29	30		

MAY

S	M	T	W	T	F	S
					1	2
3	4	5	6	7	8	9
10	11	12	13	14	15	16
17	18	19	20	21	22	23
24/31	25	26	27	28	29	30

SOMETIMES I FEEL SELF-CONSCIOUS BECAUSE MY BRAIN IS SO TINY.
S. Adams
HERE, LET ME REACH IN MY EAR AND PULL IT OUT.
8/26 © 1995 United Feature Syndicate, Inc. (NYC)
I THINK THAT'S EAR WAX, BOB.
MAYBE. BUT I'M PUTTING IT BACK JUST IN CASE.

I'M REALLY DATING MYSELF . . .

MAY 4-10

4 MONDAY

5 TUESDAY

6 WEDNESDAY

7 THURSDAY

8 FRIDAY

9 SATURDAY

10 SUNDAY

Mother's Day

MAY

S	M	T	W	T	F	S
					1	2
3	4	5	6	7	8	9
10	11	12	13	14	15	16
17	18	19	20	21	22	23
24/31	25	26	27	28	29	30

WALLY, YOU JUST SENT ME THE SAME E-MAIL YOU SENT LAST WEEK.
I'M RERUNNING THE "BEST OF WALLY" WHILE I'M ON IN-CUBE SABBATICAL.
HOW LONG IS YOUR SABBATICAL?
SIX MONTHS SO FAR, AND YOU'RE THE FIRST TO NOTICE.
S. Adams
2/15 © 1995 United Feature Syndicate, Inc. (NYC)

DOGBERT Answers My Mail

Dear Mister Adams:

My friend Raquel wrote an e-mail to you and got a personal response. But when I wrote I got what appears to be an impersonal form letter. What's the story?

—Bernadette

Dear Writer,

Thank you for your letter. Your comments are always appreciated. Have a nice day.

—DOGBERT

CLUES FOR THE CLUELESS . . .

MAY 11-17

11
MONDAY

12
TUESDAY

13
WEDNESDAY

14
THURSDAY

15
FRIDAY

16
SATURDAY

Armed Forces Day

17
SUNDAY

MAY

S	M	T	W	T	F	S
					1	2
3	4	5	6	7	8	9
10	11	12	13	14	15	16
17	18	19	20	21	22	23
24/31	25	26	27	28	29	30

AS DIRECTOR OF HUMAN RESOURCES I HAVE DEVELOPED A POLICY FOR HANDLING THE EMPLOYEES WHO COMPLAIN.
S. Adams
IT'S A BIG HOLE. I'LL TRICK THE WHINERS INTO GETTING IN IT. AND THEN I'LL COVER THEM WITH SAND.
10/13 © 1995 United Feature Syndicate, Inc.(NYC)
I DON'T SEE HOW THIS COULD POSSIBLY WORK.
THERE'S A DETAILED EXPLANATION AT THE BOTTOM OF THE HOLE.

TOP SECRET . . .

MAY 18-24

18
MONDAY

Victoria Day (Canada)

19
TUESDAY

20
WEDNESDAY

21
THURSDAY

22
FRIDAY

23
SATURDAY

24
SUNDAY

MAY

S	M	T	W	T	F	S
					1	2
3	4	5	6	7	8	9
10	11	12	13	14	15	16
17	18	19	20	21	22	23
24/31	25	26	27	28	29	30

THANK YOU FOR COMING TO THE "ISO 9000" PROJECT KICK-OFF MEETING.
EACH OF YOU WAS HAND-PICKED BY YOUR MANAGER FOR THIS PROJECT BECAUSE...
WELL... NEVER MIND WHY.
S. Adams
12-7
© 1994 United Feature Syndicate, Inc.

BIG THINGS COMING MY WAY . . .

MAY 25-31

25
MONDAY

Memorial Day

26
TUESDAY

27
WEDNESDAY

28
THURSDAY

29
FRIDAY

30
SATURDAY

31
SUNDAY

MAY

S	M	T	W	T	F	S
					1	2
3	4	5	6	7	8	9
10	11	12	13	14	15	16
17	18	19	20	21	22	23
24/31	25	26	27	28	29	30

EXCUSE ME... I'M ONLY AN INTERN, BUT MAY I MAKE A SUGGESTION?
S. Adams
LET'S FORM MULTI-DISCIPLINARY TASK FORCES TO REENGINEER OUR CORE PROCESSES UNTIL WE'RE A WORLD CLASS ORGANIZATION!
12-17
© 1994 United Feature Syndicate, Inc.
SOUNDS GOOD. GO DO IT.
I'M MORE OF AN IDEA RAT.

START IGNORING IMMEDIATELY . . .

JUNE 1-7

1
MONDAY

2
TUESDAY

3
WEDNESDAY

4
THURSDAY

5
FRIDAY

6
SATURDAY

7
SUNDAY

JUNE

S	M	T	W	T	F	S
	1	2	3	4	5	6
7	8	9	10	11	12	13
14	15	16	17	18	19	20
21	22	23	24	25	26	27
28	29	30				

DILBERT'S EXPENSE VOUCHER
YOU SPENT NEARLY $10 PER DAY ON MEALS DURING YOUR TRIP.
S.Adams
THE TRAVEL GUIDELINES REQUIRE YOU TO STUN A PIGEON WITH YOUR BRIEFCASE ON THE WAY TO THE HOTEL THEN FRY IT UP ON YOUR TRAVEL IRON.
8/24 © 1995 United Feature Syndicate, Inc. (NYC)
I TRIED...BUT IT WAS TAKING SO LONG.
TRY THE "WOOL" SETTING.

What Does It Take to Become a Famous Cartoonist?

Some people have suggested it takes a traumatic childhood or a blow to the head or abduction by sadistic aliens. In fact, it takes all three. My advice to aspiring cartoonists who would compete with me is to get the blow to the head during childhood (which is also traumatic) then use hypnosis to uncover the memories of your alien abduction. It's that easy.

—S.A.

AVOID AT ALL COSTS . . .

JUNE 8-14

8
MONDAY

9
TUESDAY

10
WEDNESDAY

11
THURSDAY

12
FRIDAY

13
SATURDAY

14
SUNDAY

Flag Day

JUNE

S	M	T	W	T	F	S
	1	2	3	4	5	6
7	8	9	10	11	12	13
14	15	16	17	18	19	20
21	22	23	24	25	26	27
28	29	30				

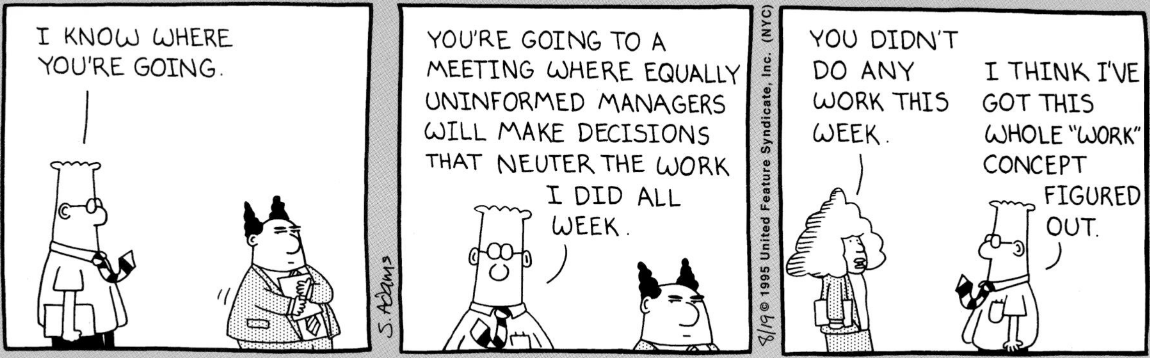
I KNOW WHERE YOU'RE GOING.
YOU'RE GOING TO A MEETING WHERE EQUALLY UNINFORMED MANAGERS WILL MAKE DECISIONS THAT NEUTER THE WORK I DID ALL WEEK.
YOU DIDN'T DO ANY WORK THIS WEEK.
I THINK I'VE GOT THIS WHOLE "WORK" CONCEPT FIGURED OUT.
S. Adams

HOW **MY** WEEK IS GOING . . .

JUNE 15-21

15
MONDAY

16
TUESDAY

17
WEDNESDAY

18
THURSDAY

19
FRIDAY

20
SATURDAY

21
SUNDAY

Father's Day

JUNE

S	M	T	W	T	F	S
	1	2	3	4	5	6
7	8	9	10	11	12	13
14	15	16	17	18	19	20
21	22	23	24	25	26	27
28	29	30				

ALICE IS SITTING IN FOR THE BOSS!
PRODUCTIVITY AT LAST!!!
EFFICIENCY! YES!!
AS LONG AS SHE DOESN'T GET AN ATTITUDE...
S.Adams
9/28 © 1995 United Feature Syndicate, Inc.(NYC)

DAY FILLER . . .

JUNE 22-28

22
MONDAY

23
TUESDAY

24
WEDNESDAY

25
THURSDAY

26
FRIDAY

27
SATURDAY

28
SUNDAY

JUNE

S	M	T	W	T	F	S
	1	2	3	4	5	6
7	8	9	10	11	12	13
14	15	16	17	18	19	20
21	22	23	24	25	26	27
28	29	30				

THAT'S AN INTERESTING SUGGESTION, WALLY. BUT IF IT'S A GOOD IDEA, WHY AREN'T OTHER COMPANIES DOING IT?
S. Adams
CAN YOU IMAGINE IN YOUR WILDEST DREAMS THAT MAYBE, JUST MAYBE I HAD A GOOD IDEA THAT NOBODY ELSE THOUGHT OF?!!
7/18 © 1995 United Feature Syndicate, Inc. (NYC)
YOU MUST HAVE SEEN IT IN A BOOK.
THANKS FOR THE CONFIDENCE IN MY ABILITIES.
YOU READ A BOOK?

OH, YEAH . . .

JUN 29- JUL 5

29
MONDAY

30
TUESDAY

1
WEDNESDAY

Canada Day

2
THURSDAY

3
FRIDAY

4
SATURDAY

Independence Day

5
SUNDAY

JUNE

S	M	T	W	T	F	S
	1	2	3	4	5	6
7	8	9	10	11	12	13
14	15	16	17	18	19	20
21	22	23	24	25	26	27
28	29	30				

JULY

S	M	T	W	T	F	S
			1	2	3	4
5	6	7	8	9	10	11
12	13	14	15	16	17	18
19	20	21	22	23	24	25
26	27	28	29	30	31	

WHAT'S THE HAT FOR, WALLY?
IT'S A NEW SAFETY RULE. I THINK IT'S STUPID.
S. Adams
THE E-MAIL FROM HUMAN RESOURCES SAID ALL SHORT EMPLOYEES MUST WEAR THESE TO IMPROVE VISIBILITY WHILE IN THE CUBICLE AISLES.
6/2 © 1995 United Feature Syndicate, Inc. (NYC)
HR SHOULD CHANGE THEIR PASSWORD ONCE IN A WHILE.
I'LL BET WE CAN MAKE HIM WEAR ALUMINUM FOIL PANTS

HOO
THRO

JULY 6-12

6
MONDAY

7
TUESDAY

8
WEDNESDAY

9
THURSDAY

10
FRIDAY

11
SATURDAY

12
SUNDAY

JULY

S	M	T	W	T	F	S
			1	2	3	4
5	6	7	8	9	10	11
12	13	14	15	16	17	18
19	20	21	22	23	24	25
26	27	28	29	30	31	

WE NEED TO FINISH YOUR PROGRAM TWICE AS FAST, SO I'M ADDING A PERSON TO HELP YOU.
S. Adams
YOU MIGHT NEED TO TRAIN HIM A LITTLE BEFORE HE'S PRODUCTIVE.
WARNING! WARNING! DR. SMITH
3-7 © 1995 United Feature Syndicate, Inc. (NYC)
TELL ME AGAIN WHAT THE BIG GLOWING THING IS.

Unscientific DILBERT Survey Results

In an actual (albeit unscientific) survey of DNRC members, the following question was posed:

"If you had a chance to hit your boss in the back of the head with one of the following objects, with no risk of getting caught, which would you choose?"

Here are the results.

19% Large bean burrito

17% Nerf ball

14% Ripe melon

13% Framed certificate of appreciation

13% The outdated computer you are forced to use

8% All of your coworkers, bound by duct tape and flung from a huge catapult

7% Your last performance review, including the six-hundred-pound file cabinet it's kept in

7% Ford Pinto with a full tank of gas (just to see what all the hype was about)

DUE WHEN?

JULY 13-19

13
MONDAY

14
TUESDAY

15
WEDNESDAY

16
THURSDAY

17
FRIDAY

18
SATURDAY

19
SUNDAY

JULY

S	M	T	W	T	F	S
			1	2	3	4
5	6	7	8	9	10	11
12	13	14	15	16	17	18
19	20	21	22	23	24	25
26	27	28	29	30	31	

RECORDS RETENTION
S. Adams
THESE VALUABLE DOCUMENTS SHOULD BE STORED FOR FIVE YEARS.
9/2 © 1995 United Feature Syndicate, Inc.(NYC)
THIS JOB GOT SO MUCH EASIER WHEN I REALIZED THAT NOBODY EVER ASKS FOR ANYTHING BACK.

UH-OH . . .

JULY 20-26

20
MONDAY

21
TUESDAY

22
WEDNESDAY

23
THURSDAY

24
FRIDAY

25
SATURDAY

26
SUNDAY

JULY

S	M	T	W	T	F	S
			1	2	3	4
5	6	7	8	9	10	11
12	13	14	15	16	17	18
19	20	21	22	23	24	25
26	27	28	29	30	31	

WE'VE BEEN HAVING A PROBLEM WITH BLACK-OUTS. THE OFFICE LIGHTS ARE CONTROLLED BY MOTION DETECTORS.
S. Adams
I HIRED A TEMP TO WALK AROUND AND FLAP HIS ARMS SO THE LIGHTS WON'T GO OFF.
2/22 © 1995 United Feature Syndicate, Inc. (NYC)
ANOTHER JOURNALISM MAJOR ENTERS THE WORKFORCE.
IT SEEMS LIKE A WASTE. MAYBE HE COULD FAN US.

FOR A BETTER LIFE . . .

JUL 27-
AUG 2

27
MONDAY

28
TUESDAY

29
WEDNESDAY

30
THURSDAY

31
FRIDAY

1
SATURDAY

2
SUNDAY

JULY

S	M	T	W	T	F	S
			1	2	3	4
5	6	7	8	9	10	11
12	13	14	15	16	17	18
19	20	21	22	23	24	25
26	27	28	29	30	31	

AUGUST

S	M	T	W	T	F	S
						1
2	3	4	5	6	7	8
9	10	11	12	13	14	15
16	17	18	19	20	21	22
23/30	24/31	25	26	27	28	29

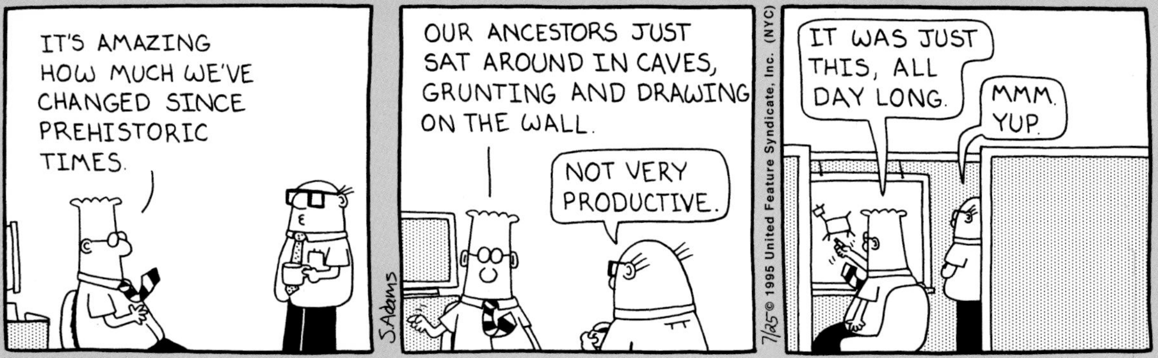
IT'S AMAZING HOW MUCH WE'VE CHANGED SINCE PREHISTORIC TIMES.
OUR ANCESTORS JUST SAT AROUND IN CAVES, GRUNTING AND DRAWING ON THE WALL.
NOT VERY PRODUCTIVE.
S.Adams
7/25 © 1995 United Feature Syndicate, Inc. (NYC)
IT WAS JUST THIS, ALL DAY LONG.
MMM. YUP.

MEETINGS TO POSTPONE . . .

AUGUST 3-9

3 MONDAY

4 TUESDAY

5 WEDNESDAY

6 THURSDAY

7 FRIDAY

8 SATURDAY

9 SUNDAY

AUGUST

S	M	T	W	T	F	S
						1
2	3	4	5	6	7	8
9	10	11	12	13	14	15
16	17	18	19	20	21	22
23/30	24/31	25	26	27	28	29

I HIRED RENOWNED PSYCHOLOGIST DOGBERT TO HELP US ACHIEVE PEAK PERFORMANCE IN TEAMWORK.
S. Adams
PEAK PERFORMANCE IS SOMEWHAT RELATIVE. YOU'RE A HIGHLY DYSFUNCTIONAL TEAM,
SO WE MUST SET REALISTIC GOALS.
6/6 © 1995 United Feature Syndicate, Inc. (NYC)
WHAT WOULD BE A REALISTIC GOAL FOR US?
I THINK I CAN POSTPONE CANNIBALISM.

DNRC Secret Hand Signal

1. Make a fist, simulating Dogbert's roundish body.
2. Extend the pinky finger, simulating Dogbert's tail.
3. Wag pinky three times The fist should be roughly waist high, in "joystick" position. Optionally, you may say

BUHWAHAHAH!!!

while giving the sign.

PLANS FOR WORLD DOMINATION. . .

AUGUST 10-16

10
MONDAY

11
TUESDAY

12
WEDNESDAY

13
THURSDAY

14
FRIDAY

15
SATURDAY

16
SUNDAY

AUGUST

S	M	T	W	T	F	S
						1
2	3	4	5	6	7	8
9	10	11	12	13	14	15
16	17	18	19	20	21	22
23/30	24/31	25	26	27	28	29

DOGBERT THE PR CONSULTANT
YOU SHIPPED KEYBOARDS WITH NO LETTER "Q." THE PUBLIC WANTS SOMEBODY TO TAKE RESPONSIBILITY.
S. Adams
OOH OOH PICK ME PICK ME!!
4-14 © 1995 United Feature Syndicate, Inc. (NYC)
RESPONSIBILITY MEANS BLAME.
GREAT... IT'S LIKE THE TIME I GOT BURNED ON THAT "OPPORTUNITY" ASSIGNMENT.

ON-LINE THIS WEEK . . .

AUGUST 17-23

17
MONDAY

18
TUESDAY

19
WEDNESDAY

20
THURSDAY

21
FRIDAY

22
SATURDAY

23
SUNDAY

AUGUST

S	M	T	W	T	F	S
						1
2	3	4	5	6	7	8
9	10	11	12	13	14	15
16	17	18	19	20	21	22
23/30	24/31	25	26	27	28	29

YOU CAN CREATE THE ILLUSION THAT YOU WORK LONG HOURS BY LEAVING VOICE MAILS FOR YOUR BOSS AT 4 A.M.
S. Adams
HI, THIS IS DILBERT. IT'S 4 A.M. AND I'M IN MY UNDERWEAR AND I THOUGHT OF YOU... OOPS... ERASE... OOPS...
BEEP BEEP
5/24 © 1995 United Feature Syndicate, Inc. (NYC)
DID YOU JUST SEND AN OBSCENE MESSAGE TO YOUR BOSS?
NO... I THINK I HIT THE GROUP CODE.

I'M SUPPOSED TO REMEMBER . . .

AUGUST 24-30

24 MONDAY

25 TUESDAY

26 WEDNESDAY

27 THURSDAY

28 FRIDAY

29 SATURDAY

30 SUNDAY

AUGUST

S	M	T	W	T	F	S
						1
2	3	4	5	6	7	8
9	10	11	12	13	14	15
16	17	18	19	20	21	22
23/30	24/31	25	26	27	28	29

WHAT DID YOU BRING TO READ?
IT'S A BOOK OF TIPS FOR MY NEW COMPUTER GOLF GAME.
S. Adams
SO... YOU'RE READING A BOOK... ABOUT A COMPUTER SIMULATION... OF AN ACTIVITY THAT'S ALMOST A SPORT...
7/17 © 1995 United Feature Syndicate, Inc. (NYC)
THAT'S ABOUT AS CLOSE AS YOU CAN GET TO BEING A NON-ORGANIC LIFE FORM.
THIS CHAPTER IS ABOUT DRIVING THE LITTLE CART.

LADDERS TO CLIMB . . .

AUG 31-SEP 6

31 MONDAY

1 TUESDAY

2 WEDNESDAY

3 THURSDAY

4 FRIDAY

5 SATURDAY

6 SUNDAY

AUGUST

S	M	T	W	T	F	S
						1
2	3	4	5	6	7	8
9	10	11	12	13	14	15
16	17	18	19	20	21	22
23/30	24/31	25	26	27	28	29

SEPTEMBER

S	M	T	W	T	F	S
		1	2	3	4	5
6	7	8	9	10	11	12
13	14	15	16	17	18	19
20	21	22	23	24	25	26
27	28	29	30			

I NEED TO THINK "OUTSIDE THE BOX" TO COME UP WITH A CREATIVE DESIGN...
I PUSH MY CHAIR INTO THE HALLWAY TO CHANGE MY VIEWPOINT AND STIMULATE MY CREATIVE JUICES.
S. Adams
9/9 © 1995 United Feature Syndicate, Inc.(NYC)
SUDDENLY MY JUICE DRIES UP.
YOU'RE A FIRE HAZARD. DO YOUR THINKING INSIDE YOUR BOX.

WHAT PROJECT?

SEPTEMBER 7-13

7 MONDAY

Labor Day

8 TUESDAY

9 WEDNESDAY

10 THURSDAY

11 FRIDAY

12 SATURDAY

13 SUNDAY

SEPTEMBER

S	M	T	W	T	F	S
		1	2	3	4	5
6	7	8	9	10	11	12
13	14	15	16	17	18	19
20	21	22	23	24	25	26
27	28	29	30			

CATBERT THE HR DIRECTOR
HERE'S THE NEW ORG CHART. MAYBE YOU'RE ON IT AND MAYBE NOT.
S.Adams
OOH! NICE TRY! SO CLOSE. TOO BAD.
3-21 © 1995 United Feature Syndicate, Inc. (NYC)
IT'S FUN TO PLAY WITH THEM BEFORE DOWNSIZING THEM.

Life after Hell

Everybody asks me what my life is like now that I've left the cubicle hell of my day job. My masseuse and manicurist asked yesterday. My chauffeur won't shut up about it. And now that they've stopped using my estate to shoot that Hawaiian Tropic commercial, I have an opportunity to tell you what it's like to be a famous cartoonist who doesn't have to "punch the clock" anymore.

It's pretty nice.

—S.A.

PRETEND TO DO . . .

SEPTEMBER 14-20

14
MONDAY

15
TUESDAY

16
WEDNESDAY

17
THURSDAY

18
FRIDAY

19
SATURDAY

20
SUNDAY

SEPTEMBER

S	M	T	W	T	F	S
		1	2	3	4	5
6	7	8	9	10	11	12
13	14	15	16	17	18	19
20	21	22	23	24	25	26
27	28	29	30			

I RECOMMEND STANDARDIZING ON ONE TYPE OF COMPUTER FOR THE OFFICE.
S. Adams
WE MUST IDENTIFY AND ELIMINATE THE DEVIANT USERS OF MACINTOSH, UNIX AND . . . GOD HELP US . . . OS/2 WARP.
6/22 © 1995 United Feature Syndicate, Inc. (NYC)
THE HOLY WARS BEGIN
DON'T LIE TO ME, GUSTAV! YOU'RE A STINKIN' MAC USER!!

I JUST REALIZED . . .

SEPTEMBER 21-27

21 MONDAY

Rosh Hashanah

22 TUESDAY

23 WEDNESDAY

24 THURSDAY

25 FRIDAY

26 SATURDAY

27 SUNDAY

SEPTEMBER

S	M	T	W	T	F	S
		1	2	3	4	5
6	7	8	9	10	11	12
13	14	15	16	17	18	19
20	21	22	23	24	25	26
27	28	29	30			

I THINK YOU LIKE THAT COMPUTER MORE THAN YOU LIKE ME.
THAT'S NOT TRUE, LIZ. I DO NOT LIKE THAT COMPUTER MORE THAN I LIKE YOU.
PLEASE, PLEASE DON'T ASK ABOUT THE LAPTOP.
"THAT" COMPUTER?
S.Adams
7/12 © 1995 United Feature Syndicate, Inc. (NYC)

CLUES FOR THE CLUELESS . . .

SEPT 28-OCT 4

28
MONDAY

29
TUESDAY

30
WEDNESDAY

Yom Kippur

1
THURSDAY

2
FRIDAY

3
SATURDAY

4
SUNDAY

SEPTEMBER

S	M	T	W	T	F	S
		1	2	3	4	5
6	7	8	9	10	11	12
13	14	15	16	17	18	19
20	21	22	23	24	25	26
27	28	29	30			

OCTOBER

S	M	T	W	T	F	S
				1	2	3
4	5	6	7	8	9	10
11	12	13	14	15	16	17
18	19	20	21	22	23	24
25	26	27	28	29	30	31

I THINK WE SHOULD BUILD AN SQL DATABASE.
UH-OH
DOES HE UNDERSTAND WHAT HE SAID OR IS IT SOMETHING HE SAW IN A TRADE MAGAZINE AD?
S. Adams
11/17
© 1995 United Feature Syndicate, Inc.(NYC)
WHAT COLOR DO YOU WANT THAT DATABASE?
I THINK MAUVE HAS THE MOST RAM.

TOP SECRET . . .

OCTOBER
5-11

5
MONDAY

6
TUESDAY

7
WEDNESDAY

8
THURSDAY

9
FRIDAY

10
SATURDAY

11
SUNDAY

OCTOBER

S	M	T	W	T	F	S
				1	2	3
4	5	6	7	8	9	10
11	12	13	14	15	16	17
18	19	20	21	22	23	24
25	26	27	28	29	30	31

WELL, IT WOULDN'T BE FRIDAY IF I DIDN'T SEE ALICE WEARING HER ONE PAIR OF TAN PANTS.
S. ADAMS
I LOVE THE "BUSINESS CASUAL" LOOK FOR THE WAY IT COMBINES UNATTRACTIVE WITH UNPROFESSIONAL WHILE DIMINISHING NEITHER.
8/9 © 1995 United Feature Syndicate, Inc. (NYC)
DO YOU THINK THE FASHION OPINION OF A MALE ENGINEER MATTERS TO ME??
TWINS!

It Doesn't Hurt to Ask

A lot of Induhviduals have been asking DNRC members for unreasonable favors. They rationalize it by saying, "It doesn't hurt to ask." After DOGBERT takes over, it will hurt to ask. Induhviduals will be required to tape on their backs a cardboard tube from a roll of paper towels. The DNRC member would then rip the tube off, along with a patch of the Induhvidual's back hair and briskly pummel the Induhvidual for asking the question.

BIG THINGS COMING MY WAY . . .

OCTOBER 12-18

12
MONDAY

Columbus Day
Thanksgiving (Canada)

13
TUESDAY

14
WEDNESDAY

15
THURSDAY

16
FRIDAY

17
SATURDAY

18
SUNDAY

OCTOBER

S	M	T	W	T	F	S
				1	2	3
4	5	6	7	8	9	10
11	12	13	14	15	16	17
18	19	20	21	22	23	24
25	26	27	28	29	30	31

CAROL, THE NEXT TIME YOU ORDER MY BUSINESS CARDS, SPELL OUT MY FULL TITLE: "DIRECTOR OF PRODUCT ENHANCEMENTS."
S. Adams
DON'T USE THE ACRONYM "DOPE."
© 1995 United Feature Syndicate, Inc. (NYC)
7/14
I DIDN'T KNOW YOU WERE THE DIRECTOR OF PRODUCT ENHANCEMENTS.

START IGNORING IMMEDIATELY . . .

OCTOBER 19-25

19
MONDAY

20
TUESDAY

21
WEDNESDAY

22
THURSDAY

23
FRIDAY

24
SATURDAY

25
SUNDAY

OCTOBER

S	M	T	W	T	F	S
				1	2	3
4	5	6	7	8	9	10
11	12	13	14	15	16	17
18	19	20	21	22	23	24
25	26	27	28	29	30	31

IT LOOKS LIKE SOMEBODY IS USING BINDERS TO ILLEGALLY INCREASE THE SIZE OF HIS CUBICLE.
S.Adams
YOU THINK YOUR STATUS WILL INCREASE WITH YOUR CUBICLE SIZE, DON'T YOU! WELL, IT WON'T WORK!
10/28 © 1995 United Feature Syndicate, Inc.(NYC)
HERE'S A RAISE. I DON'T KNOW WHY.
PSSST. IS HE SEEING ANYBODY?
RRRR

AVOID AT ALL COSTS . . .

OCT 26
NOV 1

26
MONDAY

27
TUESDAY

28
WEDNESDAY

29
THURSDAY

30
FRIDAY

31
SATURDAY

Halloween

1
SUNDAY

OCTOBER

S	M	T	W	T	F	S
				1	2	3
4	5	6	7	8	9	10
11	12	13	14	15	16	17
18	19	20	21	22	23	24
25	26	27	28	29	30	31

NOVEMBER

S	M	T	W	T	F	S
1	2	3	4	5	6	7
8	9	10	11	12	13	14
15	16	17	18	19	20	21
22	23	24	25	26	27	28
29	30					

CAROL, ABOUT THIS FLIGHT TO NEW YORK THAT YOU BOOKED FOR ME...
IS IT REALLY NECESSARY TO MAKE ALL THESE STOPOVERS IN THIRD-WORLD COUNTRIES THAT ARE EXPERIENCING REBEL INSURRECTIONS?
YOU'D BETTER WEAR THE INTERNATIONAL SYMBOL OF THE "RED CROSS" ON YOUR BACK.
S.ADAMS
10/24 © 1995 United Feature Syndicate, Inc.(NYC)

HOW **MY** WEEK IS GOING . . .

NOVEMBER
2-8

2
MONDAY

3
TUESDAY

Election Day

4
WEDNESDAY

5
THURSDAY

6
FRIDAY

7
SATURDAY

8
SUNDAY

NOVEMBER

S	M	T	W	T	F	S
1	2	3	4	5	6	7
8	9	10	11	12	13	14
15	16	17	18	19	20	21
22	23	24	25	26	27	28
29	30					

WE'LL SUCCEED IF WE UNDERSTAND WHO OUR COMPETITORS REALLY ARE!
S. Adams
MY COMPETITION IS DILBERT AND ALICE, WITH WHOM I COMPETE FOR SALARY INCREASES AND RARE PROMOTION OPPORTUNITIES.
10/9 © 1995 United Feature Syndicate, Inc.(NYC)
I MEANT OUR EXTERNAL COMPETITION.
TELL ME AGAIN WHAT WE MAKE.
NO RAISE FOR YOU, IDIOT BOY.

PLANS FOR WORLD DOMINATION . . .

NOVEMBER
9-15

9
MONDAY

10
TUESDAY

11
WEDNESDAY

Veterans' Day
Remembrance Day (Canada)

12
THURSDAY

13
FRIDAY

14
SATURDAY

15
SUNDAY

NOVEMBER

S	M	T	W	T	F	S
1	2	3	4	5	6	7
8	9	10	11	12	13	14
15	16	17	18	19	20	21
22	23	24	25	26	27	28
29	30					

THE FINANCE DEPARTMENT HAS ANALYZED YOUR COMPUTING NEEDS AND DECIDED TO GIVE YOU A 286 PC.
S. Adams
THAT SHOULD BE SUFFICIENT FOR THE 3D-RENDERING YOU NEED TO DO.
6/21 © 1995 United Feature Syndicate, Inc. (NYC)
BESIDES, HOW MANY TIMES ARE YOU GOING TO DO 3D-RENDERING IN YOUR CAREER?
ONCE, IF I HURRY.

DOGBERT Answers My Mail

Dear Mister Adams:

I sent a suggestion that you should do a comic on the subject of "work." If you use my idea, can you send me the original art?

—Timmy

Dear Timmy,

Unlike some lazy cartoonists who draw one original cartoon per day and then reproduce it, Mister Adams draws an original cartoon directly onto every single copy of every newspaper. You can simply clip your original DILBERT art out of the newspaper.

—DOGBERT

DAY FILLER . . .

NOVEMBER 16-22

16 MONDAY

17 TUESDAY

18 WEDNESDAY

19 THURSDAY

20 FRIDAY

21 SATURDAY

22 SUNDAY

NOVEMBER

S	M	T	W	T	F	S
1	2	3	4	5	6	7
8	9	10	11	12	13	14
15	16	17	18	19	20	21
22	23	24	25	26	27	28
29	30					

MISTER CATBERT, THE COMPANY IS TRYING TO FORCE ME TO USE A DIFFERENT KIND OF COMPUTER.
YOU'RE THE HUMAN RESOURCES DIRECTOR. WHAT ARE YOU DOING TO STOP THIS RELIGIOUS PERSECUTION ??! WHAT EVER HAPPENED TO "DIVERSITY"??
THE LONGER YOU VERK HERE, DIVERSE IT GETS.
NEXT.
S. Adams
6/23
© 1995 United Feature Syndicate, Inc. (NYC)

YESSS!

NOVEMBER 23-29

23
MONDAY

24
TUESDAY

25
WEDNESDAY

26
THURSDAY

Thanksgiving

27
FRIDAY

28
SATURDAY

29
SUNDAY

NOVEMBER

S	M	T	W	T	F	S
1	2	3	4	5	6	7
8	9	10	11	12	13	14
15	16	17	18	19	20	21
22	23	24	25	26	27	28
29	30					

I'VE DECIDED TO GET MORE INVOLVED WITH YOUR PROJECT.
UH-OH.
UH-OH.
S. Adams
I'M JUST GOING TO ROLL UP MY SLEEVES AND PITCH IN.
10/10 © 1995 United Feature Syndicate, Inc.(NYC)
DOES ANYBODY KNOW HOW TO WORK THESE BUTTONS?

HOOPS TO JUMP THROUGH . . .

NOV 30-DEC 6

30
MONDAY

1
TUESDAY

2
WEDNESDAY

3
THURSDAY

4
FRIDAY

5
SATURDAY

6
SUNDAY

NOVEMBER

S	M	T	W	T	F	S
1	2	3	4	5	6	7
8	9	10	11	12	13	14
15	16	17	18	19	20	21
22	23	24	25	26	27	28
29	30					

DECEMBER

S	M	T	W	T	F	S
		1	2	3	4	5
6	7	8	9	10	11	12
13	14	15	16	17	18	19
20	21	22	23	24	25	26
27	28	29	30	31		

HEADQUARTERS
HEY, CHUCK'S LOOKING UNHAPPY TODAY. WHAT'S THE PROBLEM, BIG GUY?
S. Adams
ALL OF MY BAD DECISIONS ARE CATCHING UP TO ME. COULD WE DO ANOTHER REORG TO COVER MY TRACKS?
YEAH, I'VE GOT SOME BODIES TO BURY, TOO.
10/30 © 1995 United Feature Syndicate, Inc.(NYC)
"...THESE CHANGES WILL ALLOW US TO FOCUS ON OUR CORE BUSINESS."
WHOA! LET ME GET MY REORG BOOTS.

UH-OH . . .

DECEMBER
7-13

7
MONDAY

8
TUESDAY

9
WEDNESDAY

10
THURSDAY

11
FRIDAY

12
SATURDAY

13
SUNDAY

DECEMBER

S	M	T	W	T	F	S
		1	2	3	4	5
6	7	8	9	10	11	12
13	14	15	16	17	18	19
20	21	22	23	24	25	26
27	28	29	30	31		

I'D LIKE YOUR OPINION FOR MY MARKET RESEARCH, RATBERT.
ME?!!
S. Adams
I'VE LUMPED YOU IN THE MARKET SEGMENT THAT INCLUDES WILD FUNGI AND PENCIL ERASERS.
© 1994 United Feature Syndicate, Inc.
7-22
QUESTION ONE: WOULD YOU ENJOY HAVING YOUR HEAD RUBBED VIGOROUSLY ON A PIECE OF PAPER?
WHO WOULDN'T?

Would DOGBERT still smell as sweet?

DOGBERT's original name wasn't DOGBERT. It was Dildog. I changed it at the last minute before I sent my samples to comic syndicators for consideration. Remember this tidbit in case you ever have to prove you're a member of DOGBERT's New Ruling Class. It's your password.

—S.A.

FOR A BETTER LIFE . . .

DECEMBER 14-20

14
MONDAY

Hanukkah

15
TUESDAY

16
WEDNESDAY

17
THURSDAY

18
FRIDAY

19
SATURDAY

20
SUNDAY

DECEMBER

S	M	T	W	T	F	S
		1	2	3	4	5
6	7	8	9	10	11	12
13	14	15	16	17	18	19
20	21	22	23	24	25	26
27	28	29	30	31		

THE "DOGBERT CORPORATE ART SOURCE" WILL PROVIDE LOW-COST PAINTINGS FOR YOUR WALLS.
OUR MOTTO IS "IF IT'S IN A FRAME IT WILL LOOK LIKE ART TO YOU."
S. Adams
11/3 © 1995 United Feature Syndicate, Inc.(NYC)
HOW MUCH DO THE PAINTINGS COST?
SIX DOLLARS A POUND.

MEETINGS TO POSTPONE . . .

DECEMBER
21-27

21
MONDAY

22
TUESDAY

23
WEDNESDAY

24
THURSDAY

25
FRIDAY

Christmas

26
SATURDAY

Boxing Day (Canada)

27
SUNDAY

DECEMBER

S	M	T	W	T	F	S
		1	2	3	4	5
6	7	8	9	10	11	12
13	14	15	16	17	18	19
20	21	22	23	24	25	26
27	28	29	30	31		

MY ACCOMPLISHMENT THIS WEEK IS THAT I'VE BECOME AN AGENT OF CHANGE.
I FOSTER AND REWARD THOSE BEHAVIORS THAT CONTRIBUTE TO A CULTURE OF TEAMWORK.
I'VE BECOME SLIGHTLY MORE CYNICAL.
KEEP UP THE GOOD WORK, BUDDY.
PAT PAT
S. Adams
11/15
© 1995 United Feature Syndicate, Inc.(NYC)

LADDERS TO CLIMB . . .

DEC 28-JAN 3

28
MONDAY

29
TUESDAY

30
WEDNESDAY

31
THURSDAY

1
FRIDAY

New Year's Day

2
SATURDAY

3
SUNDAY

DECEMBER

S	M	T	W	T	F	S
		1	2	3	4	5
6	7	8	9	10	11	12
13	14	15	16	17	18	19
20	21	22	23	24	25	26
27	28	29	30	31		

JANUARY 1999

S	M	T	W	T	F	S
					1	2
3	4	5	6	7	8	9
10	11	12	13	14	15	16
17	18	19	20	21	22	23
24/31	25	26	27	28	29	30

1997

January

S	M	T	W	T	F	S
			1	2	3	4
5	6	7	8	9	10	11
12	13	14	15	16	17	18
19	20	21	22	23	24	25
26	27	28	29	30	31	

February

S	M	T	W	T	F	S
						1
2	3	4	5	6	7	8
9	10	11	12	13	14	15
16	17	18	19	20	21	22
23	24	25	26	27	28	

March

S	M	T	W	T	F	S
						1
2	3	4	5	6	7	8
9	10	11	12	13	14	15
16	17	18	19	20	21	22
23	24	25	26	27	28	29
30	31					

April

S	M	T	W	T	F	S
		1	2	3	4	5
6	7	8	9	10	11	12
13	14	15	16	17	18	19
20	21	22	23	24	25	26
27	28	29	30			

May

S	M	T	W	T	F	S
				1	2	3
4	5	6	7	8	9	10
11	12	13	14	15	16	17
18	19	20	21	22	23	24
25	26	27	28	29	30	31

June

S	M	T	W	T	F	S
1	2	3	4	5	6	7
8	9	10	11	12	13	14
15	16	17	18	19	20	21
22	23	24	25	26	27	28
29	30					

July

S	M	T	W	T	F	S
		1	2	3	4	5
6	7	8	9	10	11	12
13	14	15	16	17	18	19
20	21	22	23	24	25	26
27	28	29	30	31		

August

S	M	T	W	T	F	S
					1	2
3	4	5	6	7	8	9
10	11	12	13	14	15	16
17	18	19	20	21	22	23
24	25	26	27	28	29	30
31						

September

S	M	T	W	T	F	S
	1	2	3	4	5	6
7	8	9	10	11	12	13
14	15	16	17	18	19	20
21	22	23	24	25	26	27
28	29	30				

October

S	M	T	W	T	F	S
			1	2	3	4
5	6	7	8	9	10	11
12	13	14	15	16	17	18
19	20	21	22	23	24	25
26	27	28	29	30	31	

November

S	M	T	W	T	F	S
						1
2	3	4	5	6	7	8
9	10	11	12	13	14	15
16	17	18	19	20	21	22
23	24	25	26	27	28	29
30						

December

S	M	T	W	T	F	S
	1	2	3	4	5	6
7	8	9	10	11	12	13
14	15	16	17	18	19	20
21	22	23	24	25	26	27
28	29	30	31			

1999

January

S	M	T	W	T	F	S
					1	2
3	4	5	6	7	8	9
10	11	12	13	14	15	16
17	18	19	20	21	22	23
24	25	26	27	28	29	30
31						

February

S	M	T	W	T	F	S
	1	2	3	4	5	6
7	8	9	10	11	12	13
14	15	16	17	18	19	20
21	22	23	24	25	26	27
28						

March

S	M	T	W	T	F	S
	1	2	3	4	5	6
7	8	9	10	11	12	13
14	15	16	17	18	19	20
21	22	23	24	25	26	27
28	29	30	31			

April

S	M	T	W	T	F	S
				1	2	3
4	5	6	7	8	9	10
11	12	13	14	15	16	17
18	19	20	21	22	23	24
25	26	27	28	29	30	

May

S	M	T	W	T	F	S
						1
2	3	4	5	6	7	8
9	10	11	12	13	14	15
16	17	18	19	20	21	22
23	24	25	26	27	28	29
30	31					

June

S	M	T	W	T	F	S
		1	2	3	4	5
6	7	8	9	10	11	12
13	14	15	16	17	18	19
20	21	22	23	24	25	26
27	28	29	30			

July

S	M	T	W	T	F	S
				1	2	3
4	5	6	7	8	9	10
11	12	13	14	15	16	17
18	19	20	21	22	23	24
25	26	27	28	29	30	31

August

S	M	T	W	T	F	S
1	2	3	4	5	6	7
8	9	10	11	12	13	14
15	16	17	18	19	20	21
22	23	24	25	26	27	28
29	30	31				

September

S	M	T	W	T	F	S
			1	2	3	4
5	6	7	8	9	10	11
12	13	14	15	16	17	18
19	20	21	22	23	24	25
26	27	28	29	30		

October

S	M	T	W	T	F	S
					1	2
3	4	5	6	7	8	9
10	11	12	13	14	15	16
17	18	19	20	21	22	23
24	25	26	27	28	29	30
31						

November

S	M	T	W	T	F	S
	1	2	3	4	5	6
7	8	9	10	11	12	13
14	15	16	17	18	19	20
21	22	23	24	25	26	27
28	29	30				

December

S	M	T	W	T	F	S
			1	2	3	4
5	6	7	8	9	10	11
12	13	14	15	16	17	18
19	20	21	22	23	24	25
26	27	28	29	30	31	

1999

JANUARY

FEBRUARY

MARCH

APRIL

MAY

JUNE

JULY

AUGUST

SEPTEMBER

OCTOBER

NOVEMBER

DECEMBER